Establishing Instructional Goals

Establishing Instructional Goals

W. James Popham

Eva L. Baker

Graduate School of Education

University of California, Los Angeles

PRENTICE-HALL, INC.
Englewood Cliffs, New Jersey

P 13–289256–1
C 13–289264–2

Library of Congress Catalog Card No.: 78–83136

Current Printing (Last Digit):
20 19 18 17 16 15 14 13 12

Printed in the United States of America

Prentice-Hall International, Inc., *London*
Prentice-Hall of Australia, Pty. Ltd., *Sydney*
Prentice-Hall of Canada, Ltd., *Toronto*
Prentice-Hall of India Private Limited, *New Delhi*
Prentice-Hall of Japan, Inc., *Tokyo*

Illustrations after originals by Joan Orme.

Contents

v

Companion Audiovisual Materials

A set of filmstrip-tape instructional programs coordinated with the contents of this book is available from Vimcet Associates Inc., P.O. Box 24714, Los Angeles, California, 90024. Information regarding these materials is available upon request.

Establishing Instructional Goals

Introduction

This book consists of a collection of five self-instruction programs designed to be completed individually by the reader. The programs deal with various aspects of instruction and are intended to provide a set of tangible competencies that can be employed by a teacher in making instructional decisions. The focus of the programs in this volume is on the topic of instructional goals: how to select them, how to state them, and how to establish pupil performance standards for such goals. After completing the five programs, you will be skilled in dealing with questions related to educational objectives. The competencies provided by the programs should be of considerable value to individuals who are preparing for a teaching career at any level of instruction, kindergarten through college. Experienced teachers will also find that the topics treated in the programs bear upon many practical decisions that they must make regarding their instruction. In essence, then, both pre-service and inservice teachers should profit from completing the programs contained herein.

1

Organization of the Book

The book is organized around five self-instruction programs. The substance of these programs is briefly presented below:

SYSTEMATIC INSTRUCTIONAL DECISION-MAKING. A general instructional model is described that can be used by teachers in deciding (1) which instructional activities to include in a teaching sequence, and (2) whether the instructional sequence was effective. Differences between the teacher-artist and teacher-technician conceptions of instruction are examined. This program provides an overview for the remaining programs in this and related volumes.

EDUCATIONAL OBJECTIVES. This program assists you in developing precisely stated instructional goals. At its conclusion you will be able to (1) distinguish between behaviorally and nonbehaviorally stated instructional objectives, and (2) convert nonbehavioral objectives to a form specifying student post-instruction behavior.

SELECTING APPROPRIATE EDUCATIONAL OBJECTIVES. What objectives should a teacher attempt to achieve? This program provides several tools with which to answer this question. Demonstrating that mere specificity of instructional goals does not insure worthwhile goals, the program develops your skills in using modified versions of the *Taxonomies of Educational Objectives*.

ESTABLISHING PERFORMANCE STANDARDS. This program describes concrete ways of judging the adequacy of student accomplishment. Both qualitative and quantitative techniques for assessing learner competence are illustrated, including intellectual, attitudinal, and psychomotor behavior changes. You will learn to (1) distinguish between performance standards used to differentiate achievement of students and those which aid the teacher in judging his own performance, and (2) construct performance standards for objectives in a number of subject fields.

A CURRICULUM RATIONALE. This program examines a curricular system for generating educational objectives and subsequently appraising their worth. You will learn to describe the major components of that system and to indicate the manner in which each component is employed. You will also acquire skill in identifying educational questions that are suitable for analysis by use of the system.

The introduction to each program will give you the explicit instructional objectives for the program. Then the program itself will follow. Near the end of the book (pages 101–11) a separate answer sheet for each program is provided. These sheets are detachable and can probably be used more conveniently if they are removed from the book. A separate mastery test for each program is also provided at the rear of the book (pages 113–25). These too can be detached if you wish. Finally, the correct answers to all mastery tests are given in the final section in the text (pages 127–29).

Use of the Book

Since these programs are self-instructional, it is probable that you will be proceeding individually through each at your own pace. Incidentally, it is usually better to complete a whole program at a single sitting rather than to interrupt your work. Before commencing a particular program, first locate the answer sheet for that program (and detach it from the book if you wish). Then note the program's objectives and begin reading the textual material. On the answer sheet, write your responses to questions posed in frames. After you have made the response, check the accuracy of your answer by reading further in the program. Preferably, you should respond in writing, although if you wish you may make your answers mentally. So that you do not inadvertently read too far and see the correct answer before making your response, wide gray bars like the one below have been inserted throughout the programs.

The correct answers will appear immediately following the bar. When you see such a bar, mask off the section below it until you have made your response, *then* read on to discover the accuracy of your answer. (A heavy answer mask has been provided inside the rear cover.) When you have completed a program, take the mastery test for that program and subsequently check your answers.

Each of the topics dealt with in these five programs is treated in more detail in a conventional (nonprogramed) text, *Systematic Instruction*, by the same authors. Related collections of self-instruction programs, such as *Planning an Instructional Sequence*, also by the same writers, are available. Both of these volumes are distributed by the publishers of the current text, Prentice-Hall, Inc.

When you are ready, commence with the first program.

Systematic
Instructional
Decision-Making

Objective

For this somewhat general program, an overview for the four remaining programs, the objective is the following: Having completed the program, the reader will be able to generate a written essay response to the question below, incorporating in his answer the main components of the instructional model described in the program.

> *What factors should a teacher consider in making instructional decisions? In other words, describe the decision-making scheme you think appropriate for an instructor.* (15-minute time limit)

The specific objective for the program is that the reader's post-instruction responses will reflect a position consonant with the position taken in the program.

Of the almost innumerable ways to conceptualize the teaching act, two views represent opposite ends of a continuum concerned with the systematic improvement of teaching. The first of these conceives of the teacher as an artist, while the second regards the teacher as a technician.

According to the teacher-artist conception of instruction, teaching is primarily an artistic endeavor in which the instructor, much as a virtuoso, performs for his class. Instructional decisions affecting the teacher's actions and those of his students are made largely on the basis of the teacher's insight regarding the demands of a particular classroom situation.

Since endeavors of an artistic nature often elude precise objective evaluation, it is extremely difficult to assess the quality of the teacher-artist's instructional efforts. And without evaluation, it is impossible systematically to improve the quality of any instruction.

In contrast, the teacher-technician views instruction as an *observable* interaction between a teacher and his pupils. As such, teaching is amenable to accurate definition, systematic scrutiny, and consequent improvement. The teacher-technician conception of instruction, considerably more recent than the time-honored teacher-artist tradition, is essentially an empirically based position. This more recent view contends that the instructor's activities can be improved over time by gathering empirical evidence regarding which instructional methods result in the most student achievement. Whereas the possibility of improving instruction is only slight in the teacher-artist conception, improvement is *basic* to the teacher-technician view of instruction.

In the extreme, either position is probably unsound, for there are clear elements of truth in both. Certainly many things a teacher does border on virtuosity and are almost impossible to define. Subtle nuances of instruction, escaping even the most attentive observer, can have an intense impact on a class. However, even in the case of the teacher-artist, certain instructional behaviors *can* be systematically studied and, on the basis of subsequent learner performance, effectively revised.

If one were to concede that the majority of a teacher's activities could best be described by the teacher-artist conception, the possibility of improving even a small proportion of instructional situations offers tremendous opportunities to the educator. The business world is replete with instances of major corporations succeeding or failing on the basis of only a five per cent profit or loss. In education, too, if the effectiveness of teachers' efforts could be improved by just *one* per cent, the potential learning dividends to millions of pupils would be immense.

The model for teaching proposed in this program, therefore, is largely based on the notion that a teacher should be, among other things, a highly skilled technician who systematically improves the quality of his instructional efforts. A general principle of this model is illustrated by the following example:

Teacher A: "I taught well because my class performed magnificently on a surprise exam given at the end of the period."

Teacher B: "I taught well because it was obvious throughout the period that the class was vitally interested."

Here you can see different ways in which two teachers support the contention that they have taught effectively in a given class period.

1.

Which of the teachers in the above example are you inclined to agree with?

> Teacher A
> Teacher B

On your answer sheet, circle the letter designating the teacher whose claims are best supported.

Of course you may choose either teacher's reason, but the view of instruction endorsed in this program is that it is infinitely preferable to use some sort of relatively unbiased *evidence* to determine the effectiveness of instruction. It is too easy for the teacher to delude himself by subjectively misperceiving the quality of a class's response. Teacher A's reason, therefore, would be the better choice.

The example illustrates the chief focus of a four-stage empirical approach to instructional decision-making that will be described in the remainder of the program. Instructional decisions in this approach are based on what happens to the learners as a consequence of instruction. Learner achievement, however, includes not only performance on paper and pencil tests, but also performance in a variety of other situations, some far more important than test achievement.

The ultimate instructional criterion:
LEARNER ACHIEVEMENT

The first step in instructional decision-making is determining what goals to achieve.

Step One: Specify objectives.

The teacher should describe his instructional objectives. Unfortunately, most teachers talk about their instructional goals in terms which are much too ambiguous.

2.

Which of these two teaching objectives more easily permits a fifth-grade teacher to assemble evidence that his objective has been accomplished?

A. The class will learn the basic properties of our quantitative system.
B. The class will be able to transfer numbers (three-digit) in base 10 to at least two other bases.

Circle the appropriate letter.

You should have selected B, for this objective is stated in terms of how learners are to *behave* after instruction, that is, what they can *do* after instruction.

3.

Refer back to frame 2 and circle the letter of the objective which better helps the teacher decide what to do during a particular part of the day devoted to mathematics.

You should have selected B again, for this objective provides much more guidance than objective A.

Objectives stated in the manner of B make it simple for the teacher (1) to select relevant learning activities for the pupils,

(2) to evaluate the learners to see whether they can emit the behavior once the teaching has been concluded.

Stating objectives in terms of observable student behavior facilitates
1. selection of learning activities.
2. evaluation of learning activities.

4.
Which, if any, of the following objectives describes an observable form of student behavior?

Pupils will
A. learn to love poetry.
B. read current affairs magazines during the summer.
C. solve quadratic equations.
D. become better citizens by understanding the U.S. Constitution.

Circle the correct letter or letters.

The correct answers are B and C.

A particularly important advantage of precisely stated objectives is that by removing the ambiguity of his instructional goals the teacher can often be in a better position to decide on the *worth* of his objectives. Other programs in this book will undertake a more careful analysis of how to state objectives so that they are optimally beneficial to instructional planning. With that expectation, it must be reemphasized that the first step in making instructional decisions which can later be improved is to *state objectives in terms of observable student behavior.*

A second step in the systematic planning of instruction is to pre-assess the learners' status with respect to the intended objectives.

Step Two: Pre-assess learners.

Pre-assessment may reveal that pupils already possess the behaviors that the teacher had originally hoped to teach. In this case, the original objectives can be revised upward or new objectives can be substituted, saving many hours of unnecessary instructional time in dealing with already acquired skills. On the other hand, pre-assessment may reveal that necessary preliminary skills which were assumed to be in the learners' repertoire are lacking. Also in this case it would be necessary to alter the tentatively selected goals, either by deleting certain goals or by reducing the standards expected of the students.

5.

If you were the teacher of the class described below, what decision would you make regarding your objectives for the class?

The teacher for a class of slow learners has this objective: Students will be able to multiply four-digit numbers. Pretesting reveals that no one in the class can properly add or subtract two-digit numbers.

Write your answer in the space provided.

Probably the best course of action for the teacher is to reduce the standards of his original objectives. Perhaps he should limit his objective to multiplication with two-digit numbers. Maybe even this objective is expecting too much, and, because of the weak entry behavior of his class, he should concentrate on improving addition and subtraction skills.

After the teacher has modified his instructional objectives according to the results of pre-assessment, the third step in our empirically based instructional model is for him to select learning activities which would achieve those objectives.

Step Three: Select learning activities.

When planning instructional sequences, many teachers incorrectly focus on the question "What shall *I* do?" rather than on the proper question, "What behavior changes do I want my *students* to achieve?" Attention to the first question may lead the teacher to engage in activities that *seem* to be instructional, but are not necessarily so. By focusing on the second question, the teacher usually increases the probability of selecting instructional situations which will, in fact, help learners to achieve the desired behavior changes.

6.
Which of these two courses of action seems more defensible?

Teacher selects learning activities
A. according to his recollections of how his own good teachers had behaved.
B. according to several evidence-supported principles of learning.

Circle the appropriate letter.

Although many teachers follow the scheme outlined in choice A, it seems infinitely *less* defensible than the plan described in choice B.

There are certain learning principles, drawn largely from psychology, that have been shown to increase the probability that pupils will attain a target behavior. The use of such verified principles markedly increases the odds in favor of the teacher's accomplishing his goals. The skilled teacher will master a number of these principles and will select learning procedures accordingly.

For instance, one rather generally accepted learning principle is that the learner should be given an opportunity to practice the behavior called for in the instructional objective.

7.

Suppose a teacher were using the principle of providing students with practice of the behavior described in the objective. If he had the following objective, which of the two learning activities should he provide?

Objective: Learners will be able to identify previously unexamined plants with a microscope.

Activity A: Practice in identifying plants not seen before.

Activity B: Practice in identifying wide range of previously examined plants and plant forms.

Circle the appropriate letter.

Clearly, Activity A provides the learner with an opportunity to practice a behavior that is much more similar to the one called for in the objective than is the behavior in Activity B.

While there is a considerable amount of evidence suggesting that the "opportunity to practice" principle has merit in a variety of instructional settings, an elaboration of this or other learning principles is beyond the scope of this program.[1] It is recommended, however, that a teacher become thoroughly familiar with a modest number of important instructional principles, rather than being vaguely familiar with a large, often unmanageable collection of many instructional principles.

[1] Such principles are described in a related volume by the same writers, *Planning an Instructional Sequence.*

8.

Suppose a teacher *has* designed an instructional sequence which incorporates several very important learning principles. Which of these conclusions seems most reasonable to you?

A. The teacher will surely succeed.
B. The teacher will surely fail.
C. Evidence regarding pupil performance is still needed.

Circle the appropriate letter.

If you chose C, your answer is correct, for even with a carefully conceived instructional sequence that incorporates a number of key learning principles, the only way to tell whether the instructional sequence has worked is to see if there is any payoff in terms of student attainment of the objectives.

This brings us to the fourth and final step in our empirical instructional model, namely, evaluation.

Step Four: Evaluation.

Normally, when an educator thinks of evaluation he associates it with evaluating or measuring his pupils. In this four-part instructional scheme, however, evaluation is made not of the pupils, but of the effectiveness of a particular instructional sequence. The teacher examines the post-instruction behavior of his pupils to see whether the learning activities he selected have produced the hoped-for-results. The evaluation, then, is not of the pupils but of the *teacher* and the adequacy of his instructional decisions.

Evaluation is accomplished by observing the post-instruction behavior of pupils. This is why it is so necessary to specify objectives precisely and to *pre-assess* learners to demonstrate that, prior to instruction, they could *not* behave in the desired fashion.

Poor post-instruction performance by pupils generally reflects inadequacies in the instructional sequence. In such instances, the teacher's instructional plans should be modified so that in subsequent attempts to accomplish those objectives, or other objectives, better progress can be made. In other words, each time an instructional sequence is decided on by a teacher, he is essentially testing an hypothesis regarding a set of instructional events that he contends will lead to the attainment of prespecified objectives. Such hypotheses are confirmed or rejected *only* on the basis of pupil post-instruction performance. What happens if the objectives *are* achieved? Ordinarily, when a teacher's objectives have been successfully attained he ought to add more objectives or raise the standards required of the students in his original objectives, for it is possible that he could achieve even *higher* levels of student performance from his class. Of course a teacher will reach a point of diminishing

returns when by adding more objectives he detracts from the attainment of previously accepted objectives. The teacher should cease to augment the existing goals just prior to this point.

9.
For the following situation, is choice A or B the more reasonable interpretation?

Class does poorly on final exam.
A. Students were inattentive during class and should be failed.
B. Teacher should revise instructional sequence.

Circle the appropriate letter.

Interpretation B is more apt to be true.

Answer Mask

Establishing Instructional Goals

Planning an Instructional Sequence

W. James Popham

Eva L. Baker

Graduate School of Education
University of California
Los Angeles

PRENTICE-HALL, INC.
Englewood Cliffs, New Jersey

10.
How would you interpret this situation?
Almost all students score 100 per cent on final exam, having done poorly on earlier pretest. Teacher should

A. establish more challenging objectives.
B. retain same instructional sequence.

Circle the appropriate letter.

Alternative A is probably the better choice.

We have now briefly examined four principal 'components of an empirical instructional model. The scheme can be diagramed as follows.

An Empirical Instructional Model

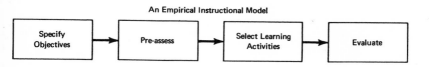

The teacher first specifies precise objectives in terms of pupil behavior. Second, he pre-assesses the learners' behavior with respect to the objectives and, as a result, may modify his objectives. Third, he devises an instructional sequence consistent with the best that is known regarding how pupils learn. Fourth, he evaluates the post-instruction performance of the learners and makes appropriate decisions regarding his instructional sequence and/or the quality of his objectives.

11.
For practice, on your answer sheet fill in the blank boxes representing the four main elements of this empirical instructional model.

The model should appear thus:

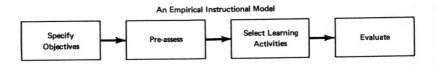

An Empirical Instructional Model

The value of this empirical scheme is that regardless of an individual's teaching style, it provides a procedure whereby the teacher, as a technically skilled expert can, over time, systematically *improve* the quality of his instruction. Such improved instruction, coupled with whatever artistry the teacher can impart to his work, will unquestionably yield learning dividends.

Educational Objectives

Objectives

In general terms, this program is designed so that those who complete it will recognize and be able to formulate operationally stated instructional objectives. More specifically, after finishing the program the reader will be able to perform the following behaviors:

1. The reader will distinguish accurately between written objectives stated in terms of student behavior and those not so stated.
2. The reader will convert nonbehavioral objectives into objectives that adequately describe post-instruction pupil behavior.

Pupils go to school to get an education. Most educators would agree on the basic aims of the American schools. They want to produce good citizens, competent workers, and sound thinkers. However, most educators realize that such "basic" aims are usually stated in terms so broad as to defy precise interpretation. If teachers wish to implement these general objectives, they must have a definite idea of what the objectives mean.

Teachers have always been concerned with the importance of instructional objectives, yet the kinds of objectives which they have endorsed usually made little difference in the nature of their instructional programs. The principal reason for this is that these objectives were stated in terms too broad and too ambiguous to allow anyone to agree upon what the objectives meant.

In the next few frames, you will see some examples of actual objectives appearing in courses of study or in lesson plans in use in public schools today.

1.

Obective: At the end of the course the student will have developed qualities of rational thought and good citizenship.

For this first example try to decide what the objective means and what kind of an educational program should be built in order to achieve the objective. Do you think others viewing this objective would reach a similar conclusion regarding its meaning and an appropriate educational program for its achievement? Answer Yes or No by circling your choice on the answer sheet.

The answer is No, for the objective is broad and permits a variety of interpretations.

2.

Objective: The student will gain an appreciation of the importance of Western European literature.

Think about what kind of educational program should be planned to achieve this objective and, more importantly, how one could tell whether or not the objective had been achieved. Do you think most people would agree on the meaning of this objective? Circle Yes or No.

The answer should be No, for although this objective limits the content to Western European literature, it is still extremely vague. Objectives such as these are not much help in planning instruction. Suppose a school staff wishes to determine systematically whether it has been successful in achieving this kind of objective. What types of examinations or what sort of observations of the students might help in judging whether the objective has been achieved? The same question can be asked of the following objectives: How can one tell whether they have been successfully achieved?

3.

Objective: The student will grasp the significance of the environment in which he lives.

Objective: Students will become familiar with the basic concepts of biology.

Do you think most educators would agree on the kinds of tests that would reflect satisfactory achievement of these goals? Circle Yes or No.

Again the answer is No. There would be great disagreement over the way to measure attainment of these objectives.

Unless objectives *unambiguously* communicate what the educator intends to accomplish, they are of little instructional value. In fact, one might think of a continuum in which educational objectives become more useful as they become less ambiguous.

Why are ambiguous objectives of little value to the teacher? Since educators have been writing vague objectives for so many years, maybe they *do* have some worth. Undoubtedly they have some public relations value in that the schools can communicate general aims to the public with such broad statements. But in the classroom, broad, vague objectives are next to worthless because a teacher can't make any instructional plans from them. Objectives should allow the teacher to know where he is going, that is, they should permit the teacher to formulate instructional plans for himself and his students so that the objective will be achieved. But if the objective is so vaguely stated that a number of interpretations can be given to it, how is the teacher to know which interpretation is the most useful? Yet, for no good reason, vague objectives are popular with many classroom teachers.

For instance, many teachers and curriculum workers describe objectives in terms of concepts, topics, or generalizations to be treated in the course.

The course will cover

1. the Industrial Revolution.
2. the Civil War.
3. the Reconstruction Period.

These objectives are examples of such "content coverage" goals. Further consideration will reveal that the teacher does not merely wish to *cover* these topics; rather, the teacher expects that coverage to help the pupils become educated. Such statements of objectives, then, really miss the point of education.

Other teachers and curriculum workers may state objectives in terms of what the *teacher* is to do during the course.

During this unit the teacher will

1. analyze the causes of World War II.
2. discuss the background of the U.N.
3. point out the current perils to peace.

Again the focus is wrong. Instead of planning *what* he will do, the teacher should be interested in *how* his activities influence his pupils. If the only objective in a history class were for the teacher to analyze the causes of World War II, no pupils need be present. The teacher could "analyze" in an empty room. Such statements, therefore, fail to provide the teacher with any *explicit* guidance about ways the instruction should affect the students.

Some teachers state objectives in extremely broad terms, with no specific reference.

> The students will
>
> 1. develop appreciations.
> 2. increase their interests.
> 3. develop conceptual thinking.

These objectives, because of their nonspecific nature, give little help to the systematic planning of instruction. Almost *anything* could be done to achieve them.

What then is a good instructional objective? How should instructional goals be stated so that they are of value to the teacher in selecting learning activities and in subsequently evaluating student performance to see whether the objectives have been accomplished?

> Good instructional objectives must be stated in terms of student behavior.

Meaningful and valuable instructional objectives must be described by stating how the student behaves, or will be able to behave, after instruction. The more specifically pupil behavior can be defined, the better. For when the teacher's goal is to change the student's observable behavior, a way of judging whether the objective has been achieved is by observing whether the behavior change has occurred. How should a teacher describe the way a pupil will behave after instruction? Consider the following description.

> The pupil will understand.

When a teacher says that a student will "understand," precisely what does he mean? For instance, think about the kind of evidence you could use to demonstrate that this next objective had been achieved.

The student will understand the meaning of the Monroe Doctrine.

Or this one:

The student will *really* understand the meaning of the Monroe Doctrine.

It is true that most people have somewhat similar definitions of the word "understand"; but if you ask them to be more specific, for example, to describe the kind of student behavior, even test behavior, that reflects "understanding," you'll find great differences in their interpretation of this term. For instance, some would think that the student understood the meaning of the Monroe Doctrine when he could write out a description of it from memory, or when he could answer a series of true-false questions about its background, or when he could properly identify instances where the Doctrine had been violated.

It is clear that terms such as "understanding," "knowledge," and "insight" allow considerable latitude with respect to their interpretation. Even though the term "understanding" refers to the student, it is next to impossible to tell what it means unless one further specifies what type of student *behavior* signifies understanding.

4.
In this frame, does phrase A or phrase B allow for fewer interpretations?

A. to select answers correctly
B. to realize fully

Circle the appropriate letter.

Phrase A is clearer because it describes an observable form of behavior. Phrase B describes a vague, internal type of response which, because it is unobservable, may be interpreted in many ways.

5.

In this frame, pick the *two* phrases which identify a form of observable student behavior.

At the end of the unit the student will be able
A. to differentiate.
B. to enjoy.
C. to comprehend.
D. to construct.

Circle the appropriate *two* letters.

A and D are the correct answers, for "differentiating" and "constructing" identify behavior that is observable, while "enjoying" and "comprehending" refer to internal, unobservable responses of the individual.

6.

In this frame select the *two behavioral* phrases.

A. to think
B. to repair.
C. to answer
D. to appreciate

Circle the appropriate *two* letters.

B and C are the correct answers, for "repairing" and "answering" are behavioral, whereas "thinking" and "appreciating" are not at all specific.

7.

In this frame, is objective A or B *less* ambiguous?

A. The pupil will learn his multiplication tables.
B. The pupil will correctly solve four of five multiplication problems.

Circle the appropriate letter.

≡≡≡≡≡≡≡≡≡≡≡≡≡≡≡≡≡≡≡≡≡≡≡≡≡≡≡≡≡≡≡≡≡≡≡

Objective B is less ambiguous because "solving" is an identifiable form of pupil behavior; the pupil's responses on a test would serve as a behavioral index of his solutions. "Learning," on the other hand, is one of those nonbehavioral words that is open to many different interpretations.

8.

Which of these objectives is the more specific?

A. The student will know the novels of Faulkner.
B. The student will describe in writing three literary movements of the Romantic Period.

Circle the appropriate letter.

≡≡≡≡≡≡≡≡≡≡≡≡≡≡≡≡≡≡≡≡≡≡≡≡≡≡≡≡≡≡≡≡≡≡≡

Objective B is the more specific since it identifies the student behavior that is sought, namely, written description. Objective A hinges on the interpretation of "know," which could be something as simple as merely listing the names of Faulkner's novels or as difficult as writing critical analyses.

9.
Select the behaviorally stated objective.

A. The student will be able to match the names of world leaders with their countries.
B. The concept of world unity will be treated.

Circle the appropriate letter.

The behaviorally stated objective is A.

10.
Choose the behaviorally stated objective for this frame.

A. The student will have familiarity with the major stylistic schools of English verse.
B. The student will be able to write a six-line poem in iambic pentameter.

Circle the appropriate letter.

Objective B is the correct answer.

11.
Now choose the behaviorally stated objective for this frame.

A. The student will really want to become a good teacher.
B. When given two objectives, the student will be able to identify correctly the one which is properly stated.

Circle the appropriate letter.

≡≡≡≡≡≡≡≡≡≡≡≡≡≡≡≡≡≡≡≡≡≡≡≡≡≡≡≡≡≡≡≡≡≡≡≡≡≡≡

Objective B is correct, for while it is important to want to become a good teacher, it is difficult to determine whether or not a student wants to. On the other hand, identifying properly stated objectives, as in choice B, is observable behavior—and, incidentally, will contribute much toward a student's efforts in becoming a good teacher.

Now that you have had considerable practice in identifying behaviorally stated objectives, here is a more difficult task—the writing of such objectives.

12.
Is the objective in this frame stated behaviorally?

The pupil will know the names of the five most recent presidents of the United States.

Circle Yes or No.

≡≡≡≡≡≡≡≡≡≡≡≡≡≡≡≡≡≡≡≡≡≡≡≡≡≡≡≡≡≡≡≡≡≡≡≡≡≡≡

The answer is No, for even though this is a rather limited objective, the verb "know" is ambiguous because a number of observable student behaviors might be used to reflect such knowledge.

13.
Now rewrite the objective in frame 12 so that there is no ambiguity about the behavior that would reflect knowledge of the names of

the five most recent presidents of the United States. Write your
answer in the space provided.

Look at your objective and decide whether there is an *observable* student behavior described. If the behavior of the
student can be observed while he demonstrates this knowledge
or if the *product* of his behavior—for example, a term paper—
is observable, then the objective is acceptable. The following is
an example of a correct answer:

> The student will correctly name the five most recent
> presidents of the United States.

This objective describes a student behavior that can be observed as it takes place, and thus it would qualify as a behavioral objective. Another possible statement of the objective

would describe a product, a list of circled names, that can be observed:

> The student will circle the names of the five most recent U.S. presidents from a list of all U.S. presidents.

This, too, is a behavioral objective. Most objectives involving student test performance are of this type. Other acceptable modifications of the objective might be the following:

> The student will list in writing the names of the five most recent presidents of the United States.

> When presented with five multiple-choice questions, each presenting one of the five most recent U.S. presidents and three distractors, the student will choose the correct answers.

If your modified objective was similar to these, you have prepared an acceptable objective. If your behavioral objective requires student performance on a test, it is necessary to describe carefully the type of test that will be used. Examples of the test items should be given, for it may be tempting to avoid the difficult task of explicitly describing student behavior by hiding behind vague objectives involving test performance.

14.
The following objective is nonbehavioral. Reword it so that it is behavioral.

The student will gain a working knowledge of the RCA tape recorder.

Write your answer in the space provided.

To judge whether your modified objective is acceptable, first see if it describes an observable student act or an observable product of a student act. If so, it is a behavioral objective. For example, the following few behaviorally reworded objectives would be acceptable:

> The student, when presented with the RCA tape recorder and a blank reel of tape, can record his own voice and play it back.

> The student will list in writing the seven most important parts of the RCA tape recorder and describe the use of each.

> The student will point out six control switches on the RCA tape recorder and orally describe the way each is used.

If your objective is similar to these, it can be considered a behavioral objective.

15.

Reword this broad nonbehavioral objective so that it is behavioral.

The pupil will become familiar with the background of World War II.

Write your answer in the space provided.

You must now realize how many choices are available in rewording such an objective in behavioral terms. The kinds of behavioral changes that might be made are almost unlimited. For instance, a teacher could have the students do anything from merely listing in writing a few causes of World War II to more complex behavior such as writing a documented research paper. To tell whether your modified objective is properly stated, you will have to judge whether the objective describes an observable student behavior or an observable product of student behavior. If it does, your objective is acceptable.

You should now be able to discriminate between behaviorally and nonbehaviorally stated objectives. You should also be able to change a nonbehavioral objective into a behavioral objective. Why should these skills be of any benefit to you? In other words, what are the particular advantages of behavioral objectives?

First, a teacher or curriculum planner who specifies his objectives in terms of student behavior is able to select appropriate evaluation procedures, for there is little ambiguity with respect to the meaning of the objective. Also, behavioral objectives make it easy for the teacher to select suitable learning activities for the class since he knows precisely what kind of student behavior he is attempting to produce.

Another advantage of behavioral objectives is that, since they are stated so specifically, the instructor himself can judge how adequate his instructional objectives are. He can also call on a colleague to help improve the quality of his objectives. When objectives are stated broadly, it may be impossible to improve them. Specificity enables the teacher to evaluate whether he is pursuing the right aims.

A further significant advantage of behavioral objectives is that they can be given to the mature student in advance of the instruction so that he can focus his energies on relevant tasks. He can then avoid spending his time either in mastering peripheral material or in trying to outguess the instructor. It may take several sentences to state an objective clearly, but once this is done, both instructor and student can be guided properly.

Finally, behavioral objectives make it possible for the teacher, and others, to evaluate instruction on the basis of whether the students accomplish the intended objectives. No longer need an instructor be evaluated on whether he has a "pleasing personality" or a "wholesome philosophy of life." Using behavioral objectives, teachers can chart their instructional goals and then go about accomplishing them. By gathering behavioral evidence, the teacher can tell whether he should retain or modify his instructional approach. If, for example, students fail to behave the way he wishes them to after instruction, he can change the learning activities. If students do acquire the behavioral changes he wishes, then perhaps he should expand or intensify the nature of his objectives.

Certainly there are other factors involved in good instruction, but precise behavioral objectives can markedly help most instructors to enhance the quality of their teaching through empirical means.

Selecting
Appropriate
Educational
Objectives

Objectives

This program was prepared to counteract the notion that "if instructional objectives are behaviorally stated, they are necessarily trivial." The general objective of the program, then, is to develop a positive attitude toward behaviorally stated objectives. Consistent with this general goal, the reader is given practice in using modified versions of the *Taxonomies of Educational Objectives* developed by Professors Benjamin Bloom, David Krathwohl, and their associates. The specific objectives for the program are:

1. The reader will be able to distinguish correctly between written objectives representing the cognitive, affective, and psychomotor domains of pupil behavior.
2. Having properly identified cognitive objectives, the reader will be able to classify them as belonging in (a) the lowest, or (b) higher than the lowest level of the cognitive domain.
3. On an attitude inventory, the reader will achieve post-instruction scores that reflect a positive attitude toward objectives that are both behavioral and important.

1.

Which of these two objectives more clearly communicates an educational intent?

At the end of the semester
A. all pupils will be able to list in writing at least 15 states not involved in the U.S. Civil War.
B. pupils will improve their peer relationships.

A.   B.

That is, which objective is unambiguously stated in terms of observable student behavior? Circle the letter of that objective on your answer sheet.

You should have circled A, for objective A leaves little doubt about what is expected of the learner. The second objective permits a number of interpretations regarding how pupils will demonstrate improved peer relationships and, therefore, is much less clear.

Instructional specialists generally agree that the proper way to describe educational objectives is in terms of student behavior; for when instructional goals are stated in such a way that the instructional target is an observable pupil behavior, or an observable product of pupil behavior, the teacher has an explicit criterion for determining the quality of his instructional efforts. Such precise objectives are, unfortunately, far less common in our classrooms than they should be. While broad general objectives may be helpful to the teacher in initially deciding on what he wishes to teach, these vague objectives are of little assistance in guiding the teacher's selection of classroom learning activities, or in deciding how to evaluate the worth of the learning activities he has selected.

Only behaviorally stated educational objectives allow the precise selection of learning activities and evaluation procedures. Yet, are behavioral objectives enough?

2.
Reexamine the two objectives given in frame 1:

At the end of the semester
A. all pupils will be able to list in writing at least 15 states not involved in the U.S. Civil War.
B. pupils will improve their peer relationships.

Which of these two goals would most teachers think is more important for learners to achieve? Circle the appropriate letter.

Although there might be some dissenters, the majority of teachers would probably agree that it is more significant for the

A.   B.

pupils to develop good peer relationships than to learn to list 15 states not involved in the Civil War.

3.

Which, if either, of these objectives is behaviorally stated?

A. Students will correctly add 10 sets of three two-digit numbers.
B. Students will become intellectually intrigued by mathematics.

Circle A, B, or Neither.

Objective A is stated behaviorally.

4.

Refer back to the objectives in frame 3. Circle the letter of the objective which most teachers would consider the more important.

Most teachers would probably think objective B was more important by far than objective A.

These illustrations should make it clear that stating objectives behaviorally in no way assures that these objectives are valuable. One of the problems of behaviorally stated instructional goals is that the types of pupil behaviors most easily described are often the most unimportant.

> TRIVIAL PUPIL BEHAVIORS CAN BE EASILY DE-
> SCRIBED: "To *count* to 10," "*Spell* your name," "Don't
> *spit* on Teacher," "To *live* through the day."

Significant educational objectives are usually elusive and difficult to state behaviorally. For instance, it is obviously more simple to describe the student's act of reciting the names of ten U.S. Senators than it is to describe pupil behaviors which reflect insight regarding the role of the U.S. Senate in determining foreign policy. Many educators who are advised for the first time to state their instructional goals behaviorally erroneously think that behavioral objectives always deal with trivial forms of pupil behavior.

5.
Consider these two objectives. Which is stated behaviorally?

A. The student will comprehend the meaning of turpentine as a solvent to be used with dirty paint brushes.
B. The student will be able to shape two clay figures, one of which reflects balance and one of which reflects imbalance.

Circle the appropriate letter.

Objective B is stated behaviorally.

6.

Refer back to the objectives in frame 5. Circle the letter of the more important objective.

Once more you should have circled B, for most art teachers would consider this outcome more important than any form of behavior suggested by objective A.

7.

Here is another illustration.

A. The learner will reflect understanding of Shakespeare.
B. The learner will perceive the meaning of Shakespeare.

Which, if either, of these objectives is stated behaviorally? Circle A, B, or Neither.

You should have circled Neither, for both objectives employ vague expressions that could be stated behaviorally in many different ways.

8.

Now refer back to the objectives in frame 7 and decide which of the two is the more important. Circle the appropriate letter.

You should be perplexed if you actually tried to decide on the more important objective. Neither A nor B should be selected as the right answer for Number 8, because no one can tell what either objective means. To judge which is the better objective is impossible.

9.
Suppose the two objectives in frame 7 were operationalized as follows:

A. The learner will demonstrate that he understands Shakespeare by *matching 10 famous quotations with the correct play.*
B. The learner will show that he perceives the meaning of Shakespeare *by writing an essay that describes the purpose of any given subplot.*

Now which objective is the more important? Circle the appropriate letter.

In this instance objective B is the better choice. When objectives are behaviorally stated, we can *then* decide which objectives are worth teaching.

Many teachers proclaim their instructional goals in glowing terms such as these:

My students will

A. appreciate my subject.
B. master the content of my subject.
C. become better human beings.

Yet, at the end of the semester, the criterion used to judge the students (and by implication, the teacher) is a trifling true-false test. Behaviorally stated instructional goals force teachers to be more aware of the *defensibility* of their educational objectives.

As was said earlier, it is not sufficient merely to state objectives operationally. Other criteria must be applied to judge which objectives are most worthwhile. Several such standards can be employed. All of them, however, require that *objectives be stated behaviorally in order for the objectives to be accurately interpreted.*

One inescapable criterion of great influence is the *teacher's value preference* regarding both the content of a discipline and the behaviors of learners. This criterion is usually employed unsystematically, but it is obvious that it exerts considerable control in the teacher's selection of goals. In a subject field such as history, for instance, different instructors will have different preferences regarding which generalizations to emphasize and which historical facts to use in elaborating on them. Even in more exact fields such as algebra, an examination of different textbooks will reveal contrasts in content. It is fortunate that in spite of many differences among teachers regarding what constitutes the important elements of a subject, there are undoubtedly many more agreements on the general value of the topics within a field.

Educators also vary in their estimation of the worth of certain learner behaviors that are indirectly tied to a subject, such as the previously mentioned peer relationships or good study habits. For instance, most kindergarten teachers undoubtedly have strong preferences regarding the merit of the following two pupil behaviors.

> Kindergarten child
>
> A. can tie shoelaces.
> B. uses proper toilet control.

Values regarding which pupil actions are more important can also be used to choose appropriate instructional goals. Obviously, the more clearly such values are stated, the more useful they will be in judging competing educational objectives.

KINDERGARTEN CHILD:
A. Can tie shoelaces
B. Uses proper
    toilet control

A second criterion that can be used in judging the worth of educational objectives is a *taxonomic analysis* of the behavior called for in the objective. A taxonomy is a classification scheme. For instance, many of the sciences use taxonomies or classifications of different sorts of phenomena. Several years ago a group of measurement specialists began to develop a *hierarchical taxonomy* of educational objectives that they thought would be of value to a variety of educational personnel. One use of such a taxonomy is in judging the worth of instructional objectives. A brief examination of the taxonomy of educational objectives is therefore in order.

The major divisions of educational objectives in the taxonomy are three behavior categories or domains. The first of these, the *cognitive domain*, covers all objectives concerned with intellectual processes of the learner. For instance, test situations where the learner displays knowledge of certain topics or the ability to perform various kinds of conceptual operations would be classified in the cognitive domain. The vast majority of educational objectives currently employed in the schools would be classified in the cognitive domain.

The second behavior category is the *affective domain*. This domain covers the attitudinal, emotional, valuing behaviors of learners, reflected by interests, appreciations, and the like. It is certainly a more nebulous area than the cognitive domain, but, according to many educators, equally if not more important. For instance, the teacher is usually more eager for a student to "like" English literature than to master a particular poem and learn to hate literature in the process.

The third domain is the *psychomotor domain*. As the name implies, this domain includes objectives concerned with skills such as typing, playing the violin, and pole-vaulting. There are a few psychomotor objectives in most subject fields, but in some, such as vocational training, physical education, and the performing arts, psychomotor objectives predominate.

10.

Indicate whether these objectives are primarily Cognitive, Affective, or Psychomotor by writing C, A, or P in the spaces provided.

Student
A. answers true-false test.
B. writes his name correctly in kindergarten.
C. recites Gettysburg Address from memory.
D. wants to be a doctor.

The correct answers are:

Student
    C   A. answers true-false test.
    P   B. writes his name correctly in kindergarten.
    C   C. recites Gettysburg Address from memory.
    A   D. wants to be a doctor.

The first objective, answering a true-false test, is primarily an intellectual behavior, hence cognitive. The second objective, a common kindergarten goal, is a difficult motor skill for young children, even though they know what letters they are trying to produce, and is psychomotor in nature. The third objective is a memory task and therefore cognitive. The final objective reflects a value preference on the part of the learner and, accordingly, falls within the affective domain.

11.
Classify this objective as primarily Cognitive, Affective, or Psychomotor by circling the correct letter.
The pupil will reflect his interest in the topic treated during the unit by selecting pertinent books during subsequent free reading periods.

You should have circled A, for this is an example of an affective objective which describes a learner's interest in a topic. In this instance the teacher has devised a scheme to check interest which is undoubtedly more valid than, for example, the method of asking the pupils at the end of the unit to indicate their interest in the topic by raising their hands.

12.
Which domain is represented by this objective?

Pupils will learn to translate correctly into English previously unseen short stories written in Russian.

Circle the letter of the appropriate domain.

This is an example of a cognitive objective, for the translation operation is an intellectual process.

13.

In which domain does this objective belong?

At the end of the unit everyone in the class will be able to identify the type of logical fallacy committed by writers in six complicated persuasive essays.

Circle the letter of the appropriate domain.

This, too, is a cognitive objective.

14.

Now study this objective and classify it by circling the letter of the appropriate domain.

The student will be able to ski down the practice slope, falling no more than once, and breaking no more than one bone.

This objective represents the psychomotor domain.

One of the advantages in classifying behavioral objectives according to this three-part scheme is that teachers often discover that too many of their objectives fall within only one domain. There is nothing wrong with having all objectives represent a single domain—as long as this is a rational choice on the part of the teacher. Many teachers, however, discover to their surprise that they are teaching only cognitive objectives and are completely neglecting affective or psychomotor outcomes. Thus the first advantage of a taxonomic analysis of objectives is that it can point up such unconscious overemphasis.

The taxonomy of educational objectives divides each domain into levels representing increasingly higher or more complex forms of behavior. Each of the three domains can be so divided, but the subdivisions of the cognitive domain are particularly useful in evaluating educational objectives and can help in selecting objectives that demand complex responses from learners.

The Cognitive Domain

6. Evaluation
5. Synthesis
4. Analysis
3. Application
2. Comprehension
1. Knowledge

Briefly, the types of objectives covered by each of these six levels are:

The lowest level, KNOWLEDGE, involves *recall* of specifics, universals, methods, and other items. For purposes of measurement, the recall situation requires very little more than bringing to mind an appropriate response. The other five levels necessitate some form of intellectual ability or skill, but the lowest level of knowledge requires only rote behavior.

COMPREHENSION, the second level, refers to a type of understanding revealed by the learner's ability to make use of certain material or of an idea without necessarily seeing its fullest implications. Instances of comprehension can be seen in a student's ability to translate languages, interpret graphs, or extrapolate from a series of numbers.

APPLICATION involves the *use* of abstractions in particular and concrete situations, such as the application of scientific principles to concrete phenomena.

ANALYSIS requires the breaking down of a communication into its subcomponents so that the relationship among these elements is made clear as, for instance, when a student distinguishes facts from opinions in a newspaper article.

SYNTHESIS entails the putting together of elements to form a new, original entity. Such an ability is the planning of a unit of instruction for a particular teaching situation.

EVALUATION describes behaviors in which judgments are made about the value of material or methods used for given purposes. Criteria applied in making these judgments may be those determined by the student or those which are given to him by someone else. For example, judging the quality of written essays according to previously established criteria is an instance of evaluation behavior.

While there are several advantages in being able to classify cognitive goals into each of these six categories, the primary fact usually revealed by applying the several cognitive levels to a set of instructional goals is that almost all of a teacher's cognitive goals are only at the lowest level. It is convenient, therefore, to reduce the six levels to what is essentially a dichotomy—the lowest level, and those levels higher than the lowest.

> Higher than the lowest:
>> 6. Evaluation
>> 5. Synthesis
>> 4. Analysis
>> 3. Application
>> 2. Comprehension
>
> Lowest:
>> 1. Knowledge

Even this rough two-category scheme is helpful in judging the appropriateness of educational objectives, for it enables the teacher to determine the proportion of his goals that are at the lowest cognitive level.

15.
Consider the following objective.

The learner will be able to match correctly the dates of famous events in the history of American education with the events.

Does it represent the *lowest* or a *higher* than lowest level of the cognitive domain? Answer by circling L or H.

The answer is L. This behavior involves knowledge, and therefore falls in the lowest level of the cognitive domain.

16.
Now study the following cognitive objective.

The pupils will be able to arrange in order of excellence three newspaper articles dealing with the same topic according to well-defined criteria of accuracy and clarity.

Does it represent a lowest or higher level cognitive behavior? Circle the appropriate letter.

You should have circled H, for this is an instance of a higher level behavior rather than of mere recall.

17.
Decide whether the following objective represents a lowest or higher level cognitive behavior and circle the appropriate letter.

The student will be able to associate correctly pictures of ten oil paintings (which he has never seen before) with one of four famous impressionist artists.

This objective represents a higher than lowest level behavior, for the student must apply previously learned criteria in differentiating among the four artists' efforts.

18.
Does this objective represent a lowest or higher level cognitive behavior? Circle the appropriate letter.

Learners can list in writing at least four works of Milton, Keats, and Pope.

≡≡

This is a recall item and falls in the lowest level of cognitive behavior.

There is nothing intrinsically wrong with knowledge items. However, if knowledge-level behavior is *all* that the teacher is eliciting from his students, perhaps his sights should be set somewhat higher. Many times a careful analysis of more complicated goals will reveal a number of lowest level cognitive behaviors which must first be mastered by the pupil en route to the attainment of a later, higher level of behavior. Such sequences of increasingly difficult behaviors are quite acceptable.

Now putting together what you have learned about the three domains and the levels of the cognitive domain, decide whether the objectives in the following four frames are *primarily* cognitive, affective, or psychomotor, and, if cognitive, whether they represent the lowest or higher than lowest level of that domain.

19.
Classify the objective by domain (and level) by circling the appropriate letter (letters).

The pupils will be able to sketch with charcoal a reasonably accurate representation of a windmill.

This is an illustration of a psychomotor objective.

20.
Classify the objective by domain (and level) by circling the appropriate letter (letters).

The teacher wants her pupils to show improved vocabularies by selecting from multiple-choice alternatives the correct definitions for 20 words previously defined in class.

This is a cognitive objective at the lowest level.

21.
Now classify this objective by domain (and level) by circling the appropriate letter (letters).

Students will fill out and return *anonymously* questionnaires designed to measure their attitudes toward minority groups.

This is an attempt to measure student attitude and is therefore an affective objective. Even though self-report devices have certain measurement limitations, they are probably better than using no device at all to assess affective outcomes.

22.

Classify this final objective by domain (and level) by circling the appropriate letter (letters).

When presented with previously unencountered problems in geometry, the student will display a creative solution by using already learned theorems in any manner which for him is unique, but at the same time adequate for solving the problem.

This is an instance of a higher than lowest level cognitive objective.

In summary, you have seen that in order to judge the value of instructional objectives they must be stated in terms of student behavior. Two criteria can be used to evaluate the quality of such objectives: the teacher's value preference and a taxonomic analysis.

The numerous examples of instructional goals presented in this program should illustrate that a behavioral objective certainly need not be trivial. In fact, operationalizing instructional goals permits the teacher to detect and eliminate those that *are* unimportant.

Establishing Performance Standards

Objectives

This program is designed to help teachers make explicit their expectations regarding student achievement. At the conclusion of the program, the reader will be able to perform the following behaviors:

1. When given a statement of an objective, the reader will identify the portion of it, if any, which describes a *student performance standard* (a level of achievement which enables instructors to identify those students who have satisfactorily achieved the objective).
2. When given an objective, the reader will identify the portion of it, if any, which specifies the *class performance standard* (achievement level used to judge the adequacy of instruction).
3. When provided with an objective, the reader will construct performance standards of the two types listed above, using both quantitative and qualitative standards.

Instructional planning has always emphasized the statement of objectives, but a rather recent development in educational thought is that these objectives must be described so they are of optimal help to the teacher. A good objective must be specific and include a description of the post-instruction behavior of learners.

EDUCATIONAL OBJECTIVES should help the teacher improve his instruction

---

1.
Which of the following objectives is properly stated?

In a math class, the student will be able to
A. solve perimeter problems.
B. understand area problems.

Circle the letter of the correct objective.

Choice A is the correct answer because it provides the teacher with specific guidance—he can actually observe students solving problems to see if they have achieved the objective.

62

There is, however, another dimension to objective writing, a dimension that further aids the teacher in planning and evaluating his instruction. It involves establishing performance standards, that is, specifying prior to instruction the minimal levels of pupil achievement.

2.
Suppose a teacher's objective is the following.

In a math class, the student will be able to solve perimeter problems.

Following instruction the teacher gives his class a fifteen-problem test to check on their achievement of the objective. Some students solve fifteen problems correctly while others get only two problems right. As the objective is stated, can the teacher tell which students satisfactorily achieved the instructional goal? Circle Yes or No.

The answer is No. The objective only specifies problem solving and provides no standard by which to judge the pupils' achievement.

3.
Had the objective of frame 2 read as follows, would the teacher be able to discriminate between successful and unsuccessful learners?

In a math class, the student will be able to solve ten of fifteen perimeter problems.

Circle Yes or No.

The answer is Yes. Students who solved fewer than ten problems would not have achieved the objective.

The italic portion of this objective specifies the minimal level of achievement for the students.

> In a math class, the student will be able to solve *ten of fifteen* perimeter problems.

Without such a standard, the teacher is hard put to identify students who have accomplished his objective, for as you can see, it is usually not enough for students merely to *perform* the behavior stipulated in an objective. Consider the following objective.

> The student will be able to draw a triangle.

What the teacher really means is that the student should be able to draw a triangle with a certain level of accuracy. The objective is improved if the minimal level of performance is included in the statement.

4.
Does the following objective have a student minimal level?

The student will be able to write an essay on the topic "Influence of the far left on the Daughters of the American Revolution."

Circle Yes or No.

The answer is No. The objective is behavioral but does not specify how well a student must perform the behavior.

5.

Does this objective have a student minimal level?

The student will be able to recite a poem by Frost with no more than three errors.

Circle Yes or No.

The answer is Yes.

6.

Refer to the objective in frame 5 and determine which portion of the objective describes a student minimal level. Write your answer in the space provided.

You should have copied the following italic portion of the objective:

> The student will be able to recite a poem by Frost *with no more than three errors*.

The teacher now has a way of judging a student's performance; if more than three errors are made, the student has not achieved the objective.

7.

Does this next objective have a student minimal level?

The student will be able to identify correctly, through chemical analysis procedures, at least five unknown substances.

Circle Yes or No.

The answer is Yes.

8.

Refer to the objective in frame 7 and copy in the space provided the portion of the objective that states a student minimal level.

The following italic segment describes the student minimal level:

AT LEAST FIVE unknown substances

The student will be able to identify correctly, through chemical analysis procedures, *at least five* unknown substances.

It should be clear that a student who identifies only two substances would not have satisfied this objective.

9.
Is a student minimal level indicated in this next objective?

The student will become familiar with two styles of painting.

Circle Yes or No.

The answer is No. The objective is not behavioral and therefore no pupil performance is specified. Remember, before student minimal levels can be applied, it is necessary to have an objective based on student behavior.

You may have noticed that the student minimal levels discussed so far have been *quantitative* in nature, that is, achievement standards have been set by requiring a given percentage of right answers or by limiting the number of errors.

Minimal levels can also be *qualitative*, which means that they specify necessary attributes of the pupil's performance. For example:

The student will be able to write a paragraph including a topic sentence, development by example, and a conclusion.

A teacher would ordinarily employ nonquantitative standards in determining whether paragraphs contained topic sentences, conclusions, or particular forms of development.

10.

The following objective also has a qualitative minimal level.

To repair a phonograph so that it operates according to factory specifications.

Copy in the space provided the part of the objective that states the qualitative minimal level.

The minimal level here is the following italic portion of the objective:

> To repair a phonograph *so that it operates according to factory specifications.*

11.

Does this objective have a student minimal level?

To prepare a research paper on the presidency that uses the format discussed in class and relates political and personal factors to presidential power.

Circle Yes or No.

The answer is Yes. Here is the objective with the statement of the minimal level in italic:

> To prepare a research paper on the presidency *that uses the format discussed in class and relates political and personal factors to presidential power.*

This is an instance of a qualitative minimal level. Of course, minimal levels do not have to be exclusively qualitative or quantitative. For example, the following goal has both quantitative and qualitative minimal levels.

> Student will be able to make an apron with straight seams and at least one pocket.

Specifying minimal levels is not simply an academic exercise. By doing so a teacher is able to decide how well a student has achieved the instructional objective and is better guided toward planning remedial or subsequent instruction.

Minimal levels not only allow the teacher to identify which *particular* students have achieved the stated objective, but they also perform another important service: they can provide a standard by which the teacher can measure his own performance in terms of the achievement of the *total class*. Consider the next objective.

> A *student* minimal level: The student will spell four out of five words correctly.

With this objective the teacher is clearly able to tell which particular students have achieved the goal. Yet, for the teacher to be able to make inferences about the *effectiveness* of his own instruction, the objective will have to be amended. Now examine this modified objective.

> A *class* minimal level: Seventy per cent of the students will spell four out of five words correctly.

In this case, the teacher has established a criterion by which to gauge his instructional proficiency. If at least 70 per cent of his class spell four out of five words correctly, the teacher knows not only which students have achieved the objectives, but also can state that the general level of achievement for his whole class was satisfactory. If only 35 per cent of the students spell four out of five words correctly, then the teacher would have reason to wonder about the effectiveness of his instruction.

Here is another illustration of establishing class, as well as student, minimal levels. Suppose a teacher wishes to foster an attitudinal objective in a music course.

> Student will volitionally attend a concert at a nearby university.

In this case, the teacher cannot judge an individual's response in quantitative terms, such as requiring nine out of ten answers right on a test, for the student will either exhibit the desired behavior and go to the concert, or he will stay away. In this case the student minimal level is volitional attendance. But the teacher can establish what proportion of the class should exhibit this voluntary behavior in order to reflect that he, the teacher, has been successful in promoting the hoped-for interest in music.

> Fifty per cent of the students will volitionally attend a concert at a nearby university.

It is important to note that an objective that has properly stated class minimal level *must* include student minimal level. The reverse, however, is not necessarily true. An objective could include a student minimal level, but make no reference to standards for the whole class.

12.
Which of the following objectives have *class* minimal levels?

A. The student will volunteer to recite a poem of his own choosing.
B. Students will solve 85 per cent of equations presented on a test.
C. At least ten students will be able to demonstrate a swan dive according to the standards cited in class.

Circle the appropriate letter or letters.

Only objective C should be circled. Objectives A and B include student minimal levels, but make no mention of the necessary number of students in the class who have to exhibit the behavior.

13.
Again, choose the objectives which state class minimal levels in terms that can help the teacher judge his own instructional effectiveness.

A. The students will draw five three-minute sketches.
B. Everyone in class will be able to write six rhyming adjectives.
C. Three-fourths of the class will understand differential equations.

Circle the appropriate letter or letters.

Objective B should have been circled, for it states what number of students must achieve the objective. The minimal level in objective A refers only to individual achievement levels. Objective C is not stated behaviorally, so no minimal level is present even though it appears that there might be one.

14.
Study the next set of objectives. On your answer sheet circle S for student minimal level *only*, C for class minimal level, and N for no minimal level.

A. Sixty per cent of the students will run 100 yards in less than 12.5 seconds.
B. Student will solve most of the division problems presented him.
C. Students will compose a nature poem in iambic pentameter.
D. Everyone in the class will locate 10 South American capital cities on a blank map.

Objective A has a class minimal level. Objective B has neither a student nor class minimal level. Objective C has only a student minimal level, and objective D has a class minimal level.

It is extremely important to remember that, if possible, minimal levels should be established prior to instruction. In that way they can serve as standards by which the teacher judges both his students' and *his own performance*. If a teacher waits until after the instructional and testing period is over and inspects the students' responses without any previously established standard, it is probable that he will be more inclined to accept the results as the "best" that could have been accomplished, using assorted explanations to account for his students' lack of achievement:

> "A slow class."
> "Not very well motivated."
> "Poor genes."

With pre-established minimal levels, after-the-fact excuses become less cogent, and the teacher is less likely to ignore the cause of poor student performance.

The question of how one selects an appropriate minimal level must have occurred to you. Does the teacher arbitrarily decide that eight out of ten is the magic formula? We hope the answer is No.

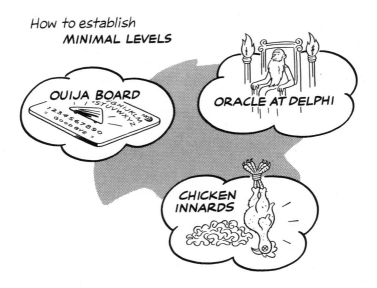

How to establish
MINIMAL LEVELS

OUIJA BOARD

ORACLE AT DELPHI

CHICKEN INNARDS

One way for a teacher to establish a realistic minimal level is to observe the capabilities of his students. If he finds, for example, that after instruction most everyone can achieve 80 per cent on a test, the teacher might consider trying to teach so that 90 per cent is achieved by all. On the other hand, he may find that his initial minimal level was too high for his students and that he may have to reduce his expectations.

In certain instances, setting minimal levels is easy. A teacher of beginning Spanish knows that for students to continue their language study successfully, they must master definite abilities in first-year Spanish, and accomplishment of these basic skills would constitute minimal levels. In other cases, the minimal level is perfection of a skill. A school of medicine would not be able to defend the practice of preparing surgeons who make acceptable incisions only 75 per cent of the time. In most situations, however, where classes are not taught in a series, minimal levels can be tentatively established, then revised after the teacher has a better understanding of the general ability levels of the students he will encounter.

15.

For a brief review, determine which of the following objectives have *either* a class or student minimal level.

A. The class will be able to answer multiple-choice questions.
B. The student will write a 300-word theme with no sentence fragments.
C. The student will perform an experiment, stating hypothesis, procedure, and results.

Circle the appropriate letter or letters.

The correct answers are B and C, both of which have student minimal levels. Now see if you can apply minimal levels of achievement in writing objectives.

16.

Rewrite the following objective so that it has a student minimal level; that is, it should be worded in such a way that it helps the teacher identify particular students who have or have not achieved the objective.

To be able to list American authors and their works.

Write your answer in the space provided.

If you modified this objective in one of the following ways your answer is correct: (1) by specifying the number of correct answers:

The student will list seven American authors and their works.

(2) by specifying authors whose identification is indispensable to the achievement of your objective:

The student will list American authors and their works, including Poe, James, and Fitzgerald.

(3) by specifying that the entire category of American authors discussed in class be identified:

The student will list *all* American authors and their works discussed in class.

17.
Rewrite the following objective so that it contains a student minimal level.

Student will be able to bake pies.

Write your answer in the space provided.

Acceptable answers could include:

> Student will be able to bake four pies.

Or you might have specified qualitative minimal levels:

> Student will be able to bake lemon meringue, coconut cream, and Dutch apple pies.

> Student will be able to bake pies that do not have soggy crusts.

If you wrote that the student would be able to bake "satisfactory" pies, your answer is not correct, for your minimal level does not provide any criteria for "satisfactoriness." Words such as "adequate," "good," and "excellent" are too vague to help a teacher decide who has achieved his objective, and without being able to tell, the teacher will have a difficult time deciding whether to improve his instruction.

18.

Now modify this objective so that it helps the teacher judge his own instructional competence. That is, add a class minimal level to the objective.

Students will answer eighteen of twenty multiple-choice test items correctly.

Write your answer in the space provided.

Acceptable modifications of the objective might look like the following:

> Fifty per cent of the students will answer eighteen of twenty multiple-choice test items correctly.

> Twenty-five of thirty members of the class will answer eighteen of twenty multiple-choice test items correctly.

> Everyone will answer eighteen of twenty multiple-choice test items correctly.

The application of minimal levels to the writing of objectives represents another way to insure that objectives function as aids rather than useless appendages to the teacher's classroom efforts. The coupling of specific behavioral objectives with *unambiguous* criteria by which to measure classroom achievement enables the teacher to gather useful information about the adequacy of his teaching and, as a result, to make changes in his instructional planning as necessary. A teacher's intensive concern with systematic planning, appraisal, and modification of his own instruction will inevitably be translated into benefits for his students.

A Curriculum Rationale

Objectives

This program examines a systematic scheme for generating educational objectives. At the conclusion of the program, the reader will be able to

1. distinguish between educational questions according to whether they are primarily related to ends or means.
2. correctly match descriptive phrases with components of the curricular model treated in the program.
3. fill in a blank diagram depicting major components of the curricular model.

As an instructional system becomes increasingly efficient, the educator's primary concerns should center on what is being taught. One of the consoling features of conventional instruction is that it is ordinarily so impotent that we don't really have to worry much about the quality of its goals. However, there should be a positive relationship between the effectiveness of an instructional scheme and the educator's concern that the right goals are being sought.

This program will examine a curricular system for generating educational objectives and subsequently appraising their worth. You will learn to describe each of the major components of that system and to indicate the manner in which each component is employed. You will also learn to identify those educational questions which are amenable to analysis through the use of such a system.

Educators at every level, from classroom teachers to school superintendents, are concerned with "the curriculum." Countless hours are spent discussing curriculum questions. There are probably more school-district curriculum committees in America than schools; and enough curriculum guides exist in school-district offices to supply school paper drives for the next several decades. Despite all this curricular planning activity, does the educator know just what "the curriculum" is? Who are the "curriculum workers"? What do they do?

A simple, and very clear, explanation of curricular planning is: An educator who is involved with curricular questions is exclusively concerned with determining the *objectives* of the educational system. There are basically two kinds of decisions that the educator must make. First, he must decide what the objectives (that is, the *ends*) of the instructional system should be, and second, he must decide upon the procedures (that is, the *means*) for accomplishing those objectives. When he is engaged in the selection of objectives for the particular segment of instruction with which he is concerned, whether an academic year or a single class period, he is engaged in *curriculum* decision-making. When he is concerned with the selection or evaluation of the instructional schemes by which those goals are to be accomplished, he is engaged in *instructional* decision-making. Thus, *the distinction between curriculum and instruction is essentially a distinction between ends and means.*

Curricular questions = Ends
Instructional questions = Means

This distinction is a particularly critical one because quite different approaches should be used in making curricular and instructional decisions. Instructional questions usually are amenable to empirical solutions, curricular questions generally are not. Without exception, the determination of what an educational goal should be is a value-based process.

Curricular decisions involve value preferences.

The very expression "should be" denotes the introduction of a set of values. Of course, one can use empirical evidence to sharpen the issues involved in value choices, but in choosing among alternative goals for the schools—and there are always alternatives—value preferences must be exercised regarding which of the alternatives are the most worthy. Such is not the case with instructional questions.

Once educational goals have been selected, it is possible to test *empirically* the efficacy of alternative procedures for achieving those goals.

Instructional decisions can be made empirically.

Given a particular goal, for example the modification of pupil behavior so that they can perform certain kinds of complex mathematical operations, the teacher can gather empirical evidence regarding the merits of alternative instructional schemes which he might use to attain that goal. One procedure can be pitted against another, and the teacher can—through a process that is essentially free of value preferences—collect evidence regarding which procedure best brings about the intended change in the learners.

The difficulty is, however, that many educators evidence confusion on this point. They sometimes try to settle curricular questions empirically and very often attempt to resolve instructional questions on the basis of value preferences. Part of this confusion stems from a basic misunderstanding of the distinction between educational ends and means.

Now you will be given some practice in identifying questions which are essentially related to ends or means. Remember that any alteration in the kinds of educational objectives which are to be accomplished reflects a change in ends. This would include the addition of new instructional goals or the deletion of old ones. In other words, any modification in the changes in learner behavior that the school hopes to produce as a consequence of instruction should be designated as change in ends. Educational means are altered when for identical instructional objectives different procedures for achieving them are introduced.

1.

Is this next question related primarily to ends or means?

Is the acquisition of a positive attitude toward elementary school mathematics (as reflected by the selection of mathematics electives in secondary school) helped or hindered by the frequent use of "brain teaser" problems in fifth- and sixth-grade homework assignments?

Answer by circling E for ends or M for means on your answer sheet.

Since this question relates primarily to the *method* by which a goal will be achieved, and not the goal itself, you should have circled M to indicate a change in means.

2.

Now study this question and determine whether it is primarily a question of ends or means.

If we use a nongraded organizational scheme, will we more effectively achieve our educational objectives?

Circle E or M.

_____

The answer is M. This question also relates primarily to the procedures used for achieving objectives, hence it, too, should be considered a means, not an ends, question.

_____
3.
Here is another question. Decide whether it is primarily one of ends or means.

Should the district's junior high schools add new social science objectives dealing with the role of minority protest groups in a democracy?

Circle E or M.

_____

Since this question focuses on the possible addition of new content, which implies the addition of new objectives, it clearly deals with ends. You should have circled E on your answer sheet.

_____
4.
Suppose you were asked to consider the following educational changes suggested by your colleagues. How would you classify these suggestions according to an ends-means distinction? Identify each proposal by circling E for ends change and M for means change.

A. Provide more oral practice for students in speech classes in order to achieve more efficiently the current goals of the course.
B. Alter the chemistry course by adding new topics during free time created as a consequence of covering existing topics more efficiently.
C. Delete all driver-education courses.
D. Have ten guest physicians speak to health-education classes in order to motivate the students to achieve the course goals more effectively.
E. Improve the English curriculum by rearranging the order in which topics are treated during the year.

You should have designated choices A, D, and E as means changes since they are primarily concerned with the procedures used in achieving objectives. Choices B and C are related to the addition and deletion of objectives and thus should have been designated as ends changes.

With this distinction between ends and means in mind, we can turn to an examination of a scheme designed to improve the quality of the educational ends to be selected. It may occur to you that the really important selections have already been made by educators in the past, so that there is little sense in even pursuing this question. After all, curriculum guides have been written in every large school district and most of the smaller ones as well. In spite of these guides, however, there is much curricular decision-making to be done. Most current curriculum guides contain instructional objectives that are so general that they allow the teacher considerable latitude in the specification of objectives for particular teaching situations.

For instance, many objectives such as the following are given in public school curriculum guides:

> The pupil will understand the forces contributing to the Civil War.

There are obviously many ways of operationalizing such an objective. Given the general goal, the instructor can choose from numerous alternatives. The danger is that if the teacher selects these alternatives "off the top of his head," he may choose unwisely.

Of all the schemes available for selecting objectives, the most widely accepted is the one developed a number of years ago by Professor Ralph Tyler.[1] This system for making curricular decisions, often referred to as the "Tyler Rationale," offers an approach to the selection of objectives that is designed to make the educator more systematic and circumspect in the selection. Schematically, the Tyler Rationale can be depicted as follows.

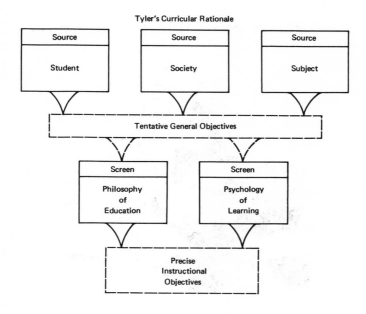

Tyler's Curricular Rationale

[1] Ralph W. Tyler, *Basic Principles of Curriculum and Instruction.* Chicago: The University of Chicago Press, 1950.

According to this scheme, the curriculum maker looks to three sources—student, society, and subject—from which he derives general, tentative objectives. He then screens these tentative goals by means of his philosophy of education and a psychology of learning. Next, he states the objectives that survive this screening in precise terms of measurable learner behaviors. These precise objectives serve as the ends for which the teacher designs effective instructional means.

Let's look more closely at each of the components of this model. Instead of sitting down to think randomly about what objectives should be taught, Tyler suggests that one consider three potential sources of objectives, starting with a careful study of the student.

Study the student: his *needs* and his *interests*.

By studying the learners themselves, particularly their needs and interests, the curriculum maker may discover worthwhile objectives that might otherwise not have occurred to him. If he can gather information about the current status of the learners and compare that status with some conception of an acceptable norm, then any difference between the two he can generally refer to as a need. An investigation of elementary school youngsters in a particular community may reveal dietary deficiencies and a need with respect to physical condition. Such a need might suggest an objective in health education. Similarly, by studying the current status of students with respect to how much they know about municipal government, the curriculum maker might discover needs that could be met by certain objectives in social science courses.

Determine student needs.

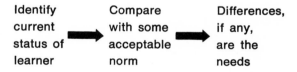

| Identify current status of learner | → | Compare with some acceptable norm | → | Differences, if any, are the needs |

It can be seen, then, that there must first be some kind of investigation to determine the learner's current status. The more systematic this investigation is, the better. However, it would be preferable to perform this "status check" very informally rather than not at all. Next, the curriculum maker compares the status of the student with some standard considered desirable, and identifies any differences as needs. Consideration of these needs will usually lead the curriculum maker to one or more tentative objectives. For example, in the previous illustration regarding municipal government, the objective might be stated quite generally as follows.

> The students ought to possess more factual information regarding the process of local government.

Note that the objective is not stated precisely, that is, not in terms of learner behavior. Such precision is unnecessary at this point, for the curriculum maker may subsequently screen the objective from the final group of objectives he wishes to achieve.

A second area of useful information regarding the learner can be secured by studying his interests. The general notion supporting the usefulness of this source is that the student learns best those things in which he is vitally involved. Such involvement occurs most easily when the student is permitted to study the things in which he is interested. Hence, by selecting instructional objectives consonant with learner interests, the schools can promote more efficient learning. For example, if the curriculum makers discover that a group of youngsters of junior high school age are particularly interested in space exploration, they might generate a number of objectives to match this interest. In the process of studying outer space, the students may learn all sorts of related skills—and learn them to last for a long time—because they are truly interested in achieving the objectives.

Once more, data describing student interests must be interpreted according to some acceptable norms. The discovery that a segment of high school boys is interested in pornographic literature would not necessarily imply that the school should have objectives promoting more rapid and insightful reading of such literature. As in the case of securing information regarding pupil needs, learner-interest data can be secured through formal sociological investigations or through more casual teacher-conducted inquiries such as interviews, observations, and questionnaires involving pupils, parents, or experienced teachers.

5.

Thus, when using the student as a possible source of objectives, the teacher should attend to two types of data. In the space provided, write what these two types of data are.

You should have indicated that information regarding the student's *needs* and *interests* is helpful in the selection of objectives.

Study the society.

A second source of possible objectives can be found in an examination of contemporary life outside the school. In general, the reason for studying the nature of the present society is to be able to determine more accurately the kinds of competencies needed by today's citizens. With this knowledge, educational objectives can be established which are designed to produce these competencies. Of course, arguments exist for and against the use of the current status of society as a source of objectives. However, since the society does support the very existence of our school system, it seems only reasonable to consider educational objectives based on a societal analysis.

Because of the complexity of any modern society, it is necessary to develop manageable categories for study. Tyler suggests as one alternative the following set of classifications.

Society can be studied in terms of:
Health
Family
Recreation
Vocation
Religion
Civic affairs

Investigations of the society can be conducted on a large- or small-scale basis, depending on the resources and abilities of the individuals conducting the investigations. For example, an individual teacher might analyze the vocational needs of the local community and decide that the schools should produce more students who possess the psychomotor skills required by local industry. Or perhaps a group of faculty members could systematically solicit the opinions of the lay community to find out what broad goals citizens think the schools should be accomplishing.

Study the subject.

A final source of objectives in the Tyler Rationale is based on the suggestions of subject specialists. This source of objectives is most commonly used in typical schools and colleges. Until relatively recent times the subject specialist was legitimately criticized on the grounds that his suggestions for educational objectives were too technical, too specialized, and inappropriate for the majority of students. Too often the subject specialist tended to suggest objectives that were more suitable for the training of subject specialists than for the average citizen. This situation has now been altered, and in recent years prominent experts have given much attention to the identification of goals that all learners should achieve. Curriculum recommendations of prominent individuals or groups, such as the National Council of English Teachers, contain a wealth of suggestions for possible objectives.

We have briefly examined the three data sources in Tyler's curriculum scheme. Consideration of each can lead to the identification of possible objectives.

6.
Review the manner in which objectives should be stated at this point. Should they be explicated precisely in terms of measurable learner behavior? Circle Yes or No.

You should have answered No, for at this point it is somewhat premature to specify the objectives with that much precision. You might waste much time operationalizing an objective that may not survive a subsequent screening.

At this point in the use of the rationale the curriculum maker should have a collection of general objectives, quite probably more than can be reasonably attained in the instructional time available. Too many educators make the serious mistake of "covering" too much territory. Surely they can assert that they have "covered" much material, but it is usually the case that this coverage results in little, if any, important modifications in the behavior of learners. The next step in the Tyler scheme is to rank the tentative objectives in some rough sort of hierarchy so that those which are unimportant or impossible to achieve can be discarded. This ranking is accomplished through the use of two screens.

7.

Can you recall what the two screens in Tyler's Rationale are? Write your answer in the spaces provided.

If you answered "philosophy of education" and "psychology of learning," you have excellent powers of recall.

Turning first to the screen of philosophy of education, it should be pointed out that what Tyler had in mind was no elaborate educational philosophy, replete with metaphysical postulates.

Rather, by philosophy of education he simply meant the set of values one holds regarding what should be taught in the schools. All of us undoubtedly have some primitive notions of what the goals of the schools ought to be. In the use of the philosophical screen the educator brings these values to bear on the tentative objectives and deletes any that are inconsistent with those values. Obviously, the more reasonable one's value system is, the more efficiently he can use it in appraising possible educational goals. To illustrate, an educator may believe that any concession to learner interests or needs is inappropriate because, he is convinced, "the role of the school is to perpetuate the society, not pamper the individual." With such a philosophy, that educator would undoubtedly reject all objectives derived from a consideration of the students' needs or interests, or at least demote such objectives to a low position in the hierarchy.

After using the philosophical screen, the curriculum maker should roughly order his objectives according to those which must be achieved if time permits, and those which need not be achieved. The psychology of learning screen can then be applied. A primary purpose of this screen is to distinguish between those objectives which are feasible from those which are apt to take a very long time or are nearly impossible to attain at the age level contemplated. For instance, evidence shows that it is incredibly difficult to bring about any profound personality modifications in human beings much past the first five or six years of life. Objectives, however laudable, that attempt to do so in one high school semester should undoubtedly be discarded. Educators know much less than they wish they knew regarding what kinds of objectives are teachable at given age levels. As evidence regarding this question accumulates, the psychology of learning screen will become more efficient in filtering out unteachable goals.

The order in which the two screens should be used is arbitrary. One could employ the psychology screen first and the philosophy screen second. Ralph Tyler recently suggested that the two screens might even be brought into play prior to the use of the three data sources. Although the order described in this program—that is, sources first and screens second—seems somewhat more logical, a teacher might wish first to impose the limitations suggested by the two screens, then work with the data sources.

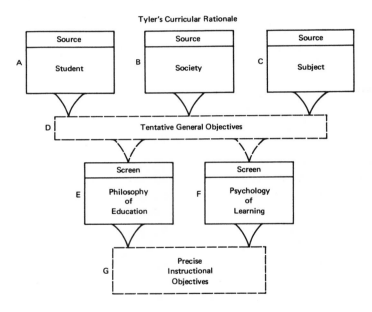

Tyler's Curricular Rationale

Regardless of the order, as long as the curriculum maker considers all five components of the rationale, he should in the end have a screened set of objectives stated in terms of measurable learner behaviors. It is this set of objectives that guides the selection of instructional and evaluation schemes.

Look once more at the schematic representation of the Tyler Rationale. Note that seven letter-subscripts, A through G, have been added. To give you more familiarity with the elements of this model, frames 8 through 14 will provide a series of phrases that you should associate with one of the seven categories in the diagram. After reading each phrase, examine the schematic diagram and then circle on your answer sheet the letter of the diagram element to which the phrase pertains.

8.

To which diagram element does this phrase pertain? Circle the appropriate letter.

A collection of loosely stated goals.

You should have circled letter D.

9.

Circle the letter of the diagram element to which this phrase pertains.

Helps discard the unattainable.

Since this activity is associated with the psychological screen, you should have circled letter F.

10.

Circle the letter of the diagram element to which this phrase pertains.

A study of fifth-grade children's television-viewing habits would be relevant.

This would undoubtedly be associated with the use of student interests as a source of objectives; hence you should have selected A.

11.

Circle the letter of the diagram element to which this phrase pertains.

A survey of the types of jobs open to high school graduates would be important data.

Since this sort of information would be most important in the use of contemporary society as a data source, you should have selected B.

12.

Circle the letter of the diagram element to which this phrase pertains.

An educator's value preferences come into play.

E is the correct answer.

13.

Circle the letter of the diagram element to which this phrase pertains.

Consulting the subject experts.

This activity is most closely associated with securing the suggestions of subject specialists; hence you should have selected C.

14.

Circle the letter of the diagram element to which this phrase pertains.

Behavioral objectives.

Since the final step in the Tyler model is the formulation of a set of precise behavioral objectives, you should have selected G as your answer.

15.

Now study the schematic diagram (p. 96) carefully, and when you feel that you know its components, fill in the blank diagram on your answer sheet.

Now refer back to the completed diagram to check the accuracy of your answers.

We have briefly examined a curriculum model proposed by Ralph Tyler. It can be employed at all levels of sophistication, ranging from a well-financed, systematic implementation by a team of experts to an informal use by a classroom teacher during an evening of armchair decision-making about his curriculum. A primary value of using such a rationale is that it forces the educator to be more circumspect in the selection of ends. A judicious selection of the ends of instruction will make efforts to find effective instructional means worth the trouble.

Program
Answer
Sheets

Systematic Instructional Decision-Making *Answer Sheet*

1. A B
2. A B
3. A B
4. A B C D
5. _____
    _____
    _____
    _____

6. A B
7. A B
8. A B C
9. A B
10. A B
11.

An Empirical Instructional Model

Educational Objectives *Answer Sheet*

1. Yes No
2. Yes No
3. Yes No
4. A B
5. A B C D
6. A B C D
7. A B
8. A B
9. A B
10. A B
11. A B
12. Yes No
13. Modified objective: _____

_____

_____

_____

14. Modified objective: _____

_____

_____

_____

15. Modified objective: _____

_____

_____

_____

Selecting Appropriate Educational Objectives *Answer Sheet*

1.	A	B		
2.	A	B		
3.	A	B	Neither	
4.	A	B		
5.	A	B		
6.	A	B		
7.	A	B	Neither	
8.	A	B		
9.	A	B		

10. (C = Cognitive,
    A = Affective,
    P = Psychomotor)
    A._____   C._____
    B._____   D._____

11. C   A   P
12. C   A   P
13. C   A   P
14. C   A   P
    (L = Lowest, H = Higher)
15. L   H
16. L   H
17. L   H
18. L   H
19. C   (L or H)   A   P
20. C   (L or H)   A   P
21. C   (L or H)   A   P
22. C   (L or H)   A   P

Establishing Performance Standards *Answer Sheet*

1. A   B
2. Yes   No
3. Yes   No
4. Yes   No
5. Yes   No
6. _____
7. Yes   No
8. _____
9. Yes   No
10. _____
11. Yes   No
12. A   B   C
13. A   B   C
14. A. S   C   N
    B. S   C   N
    C. S   C   N
    D. S   C   N
15. A   B   C
16. _____
    _____
    _____
17. _____
    _____
    _____
18. _____
    _____
    _____

A Curriculum Rationale *Answer Sheet*

1. E M   4. A. E M
2. E M   B. E M
3. E M   C. E M
                                              D. E M
                                              E. E M

5. _____

6. Yes   No

7. _____   _____

8. A B C D E F G   12. A B C D E F G
9. A B C D E F G   13. A B C D E F G
10. A B C D E F G   14. A B C D E F G
11. A B C D E F G   15. (See next page.)

Tyler's Curricular Rationale

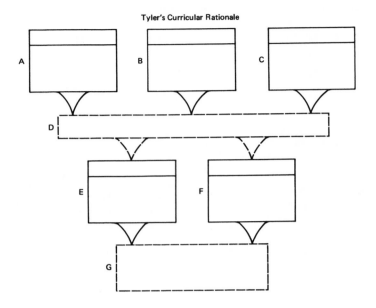

Mastery
Tests

Mastery Test: Systematic Instructional Decision-Making

Name _____

In the space below, answer the following question in 15 minutes or less:

What factors should a teacher consider in making instructional decisions? In other words, describe the decision-making scheme you think appropriate for an instructor.

Mastery Test: Educational Objectives

Name _____

Part I.   Complete this question before you look at Part II. Change
the objective below so that it is stated in terms of student
behavior. (Either make written modifications of the objective
or write out a new objective.)

At the end of the course, the student will understand the
fundamental concepts of biology.

Part II.   Place an X before any of the following instructional objectives
that are properly stated.

_____ 1.   The student will grasp the significance of the Treaty of
Versailles.

_____ 2.   The student will have an attitude favorable to English
grammar indicated by his response to a questionnaire.

_____ 3.   The student will know six verbs.

_____ 4.   The student will learn the names of the common tools
in wood shop.

_____ 5.   The teacher will list three major causes of the Civil War
on the chalkboard.

_____ 6.   The student will know the important battles of World
War I.

_____ 7.   The student will prefer cooking to sewing.

_____ 8.   The student will be able to correctly thread a sewing
machine.

_____ 9.   The student will pay attention as the teacher demonstrates the use of the lathe.

_____10.   The student will be able to develop a sense of the
cultural unity of man.

_____11.   The student will list and describe the themes of four
of Shelley's poems.

_____12. The child will develop interest in leisure sports.

_____13. The student will give indications of a desire to learn more history by volunteering to present an extra oral report.

_____14. The teacher will describe with understanding five concepts treated in the text.

_____15. The student will correctly solve all of the story problems presented.

_____16. The student will accurately learn the best-known works of Voltaire.

_____17. The teacher will help the class to solve algebra problems correctly.

_____18. The student will appreciate the key importance of algebraic approaches.

_____19. The student will include 10 supporting facts in a written persuasive paragraph.

_____20. The student will become familiar with writing an essay by using no reference but personal experience.

Mastery Test: Selecting Appropriate Educational Objectives

(Note: Both cognitive and affective mastery tests are provided for this program.)

Name _____

Taxonomy Classification

Classify each objective below by writing the correct letter in front of the objective according to the following scheme:
A. psychomotor
B. affective
C. cognitive—higher than lowest level
D. cognitive—lowest level

The learner

_____ 1. is able to choose the best of two solutions to a geometry problem using standards given by the teacher.

_____ 2. exhibits tolerance for others by displaying good manners toward those of minority groups.

_____ 3. lists the names and contributions of the five key curriculum workers as described in class.

_____ 4. properly knits a baby blanket.

_____ 5. scores well on the Minnesota Teacher Attitude Inventory.

_____ 6. uses instructional principles properly in planning daily lessons.

_____ 7. plays table tennis according to rules well enough to beat three inexperienced girls 100 per cent of the time.

_____ 8. correctly recites Gettysburg Address from memory.

_____ 9. scores 80 per cent or better on a spelling quiz.

_____ 10. displays interest in higher mathematics by volitionally attending lectures on this topic.

The following attitude inventory should be used with the *Selecting Appropriate Educational Objectives* program. Validity studies regarding the inventory have been reported.[1]

**Instructional Objectives
Preference List**

Name _____

Rate each of the following instructional objectives according to the following scheme—Excellent: 5; Good: 4; Average: 3; Fair: 2; Poor: 1. There are no "right" or "wrong" answers for this list, so please express your preferences candidly by placing a number before each objective.

_____ 1. The student will be able to comprehend thoroughly the ways in which our constitution permeates our every-day life.

_____ 2. When presented with a list of nouns and pronouns, the student will be able to label each word correctly.

_____ 3. Student will be able to see the value of reading the "classics" in his leisure time.

_____ 4. The student will be able to write an essay employing one of three logical organizations given in class which exhibits no grammatical errors.

_____ 5. The student will be able to learn the number of voters in his precinct.

_____ 6. The student will be able to list those articles in the con-stitution which relate to "due process of law."

_____ 7. Students will realize the importance of knowing the approximate date at which a given literary work was produced.

_____ 8. The teacher will cover the key tools of the chemistry lab, that is, the Bunsen burner and various types of test tubes.

_____ 9. Given a list of 10 actual municipal court decisions, the student will be able to select the six which violate key

[1]W. James Popham and Eva L. Baker, "Measuring Teachers' Attitudes Toward Behavioral Objectives," *The Journal of Educational Research*, Vol. LX, No. 10 (July-August 1967), pp. 453–455. W. James Popham and Eva L. Baker, "The Instructional Objectives Preference List," *Journal of Educational Measurement*, Vol. II, No. 2 (December 1965), p. 186.

tenets of the constitution and subsequently write an essay briefly explaining the nature of these violations.

_____10. The student will orally recite the names of six chemical compounds containing three or more elements.

_____11. The student will be able to cite some of the literary "classics" and briefly describe in an essay those features which give them universal appeal.

_____12. The student will grasp the significance of civic responsibility.

_____13. The student will be able to name the date when women were first permitted to vote.

_____14. The teacher will discuss the grammatical form of the amendments to the constitution.

_____15. The student will be cognizant of the important role scientific investigation has played in the field of chemistry and will become conversant with the relationship between scientific inquiry and the everyday life of the individual.

_____16. The teacher will help the class to become proficient communicators in written English.

_____17. Given the names of well-known novels and the names of contemporary authors, the student will be able to match them correctly in a test.

_____18. The student will be able to write an essay in which he contrasts the arguments for having a democracy or totalitarian state.

_____19. The student will learn the parts of speech.

_____20. The student will be capable of setting up an experimental hypothesis test in the field of quantitative chemical analysis so that presented with an unknown chemical compound he can thereafter correctly identify its constituent elements.

Mastery Test: Establishing Performance Standards

Name _____

Part I. For the following objectives, circle *S* if the objective has only a *student* minimal level of learner behavior; circle *C* if the objective has a *class* minimal level of learner behavior; circle *N* if the objective has *no* minimal level of learner behavior.

S C N 1. The class will answer correctly 10 out of 12 multiple-choice questions on the Roman Empire.

S C N 2. The students will compose an essay on the topic of their summer vacation.

S C N 3. At least 10 students in the class will sign up for a senior life-saving course at the conclusion of a unit on water safety.

S C N 4. Seventy-five percent of the students will understand differential equations.

S C N 5. Students will recite with no more than one error Milton's sonnet "On His Blindness."

S C N 6. Sixty per cent of the students will prepare book reports on famous social scientists.

S C N 7. The students will thoroughly comprehend at least 80 per cent of the scientific theories treated in class.

S C N 8. The students will paint a still-life study employing two-point perspective and at least three colors.

S C N 9. Everyone in class will orally recite a given Spanish dialogue with no errors in pronunciation.

S C N 10. Students will be able to match chemical compounds with their valences on a written test.

Part II. The following objectives include performance standards of learner behavior. *Underline* the portion of each objective which specifies the performance standard.

11. The student will write a composition which exhibits no spelling errors.

12. Ninety per cent of the students will be able to label all parts of a diagram of the human skeleton.

13. At least 20 students will voluntarily select poetry books from the library.

14. All members of the class will participate *at least twice* in a class discussion on foreign policy.

Part III. Rewrite this objective so that it exhibits both *class* and *student* minimal levels:

15. The student will answer a completion examination on medieval England.

Rewrite this objective so that it exhibits a *student* minimal level only:

16. The student will be able to solve statistics problems.

Mastery Test: A Curriculum Rationale

Name _____

Part I. Check any of the following six items that indicate a change in educational *means* rather than ends.

_____ 1. Rearrange sequence of objectives treated in the biology course.

_____ 2. Use new self-study pamphlets to teach the usual current-events topics in sixth-grade social science.

_____ 3. Drop health-education course objectives dealing with sex education.

_____ 4. Use increased quantities of teacher reinforcement in classroom discussions.

_____ 5. Add new goals dealing with post-World War II conflicts to the history course.

_____ 6. Reduce the number of skills to be developed in the mathematics course in order to add more objectives regarding pupils' most basic computation deficiencies.

Part II. In the space provided, write the letter of the rationale component most closely associated with each of the following six phrases.

A. Student as a source
B. Society as a source
C. Subject as a source
D. Tentative objectives
E. Philosophical screen
F. Psychological screen
G. Final objective

_____ 7. Imprecise goals
_____ 8. Free-time reading interests
_____ 9. Current vocational opportunities
_____10. Identifies unteachable goals
_____11. National Council of Social Science Teachers
_____12. Value preferences yield hierarchy of goals

Answers to Mastery Tests

Systematic Instructional Decision-Making

In scoring the response to this largely unstructured question, four points can be awarded. Give one point for any explicit reference to each of the following four items: (a) instructional objectives, (b) pre-assessment, (c) learning activities, and (d) evaluation of the quality of instruction. Descriptive terms other than these can be used to secure credit, but the main ideas must be incorporated in the response.

Educational Objectives

PART I.   The objective must be revised to include a description of observable student behavior or a tangible product resulting from student behavior. For example: student can discriminate between correct and incorrect statements of key biological concepts.

PART II.   An X should have been placed before the following objectives: 2, 8, 11, 13, 15, 19.

Selecting Appropriate Educational Objectives

Taxonomy Classification: 1. C, 2. B, 3. D, 4. A, 5. B, 6. C, 7. A, 8. D, 9. D, 10. B.

Instructional Objectives Preference List

Total: Step 1.   Add numbers by items 2, 4, 6, 9, 10, 11, 13, 17, 18, 20.
This is subtotal No. 1.

Step 2.   Add numbers by the remaining items.
This is subtotal No. 2.

Step 3.   Subtract subtotal No. 2 from 60.

Step 4.   Add the result of Step 3 to subtotal No. 1.
This is the score for the *IOPL*.

Scores can range from 20 to 100, with higher scores reflecting preferences for behaviorally stated objectives.

Subscales: Add the numerical ratings for each of the following sets of items to obtain subscale scores. High
scores on each of these subscales reflect preferences for the type of objectives used in that subscale, e.g., nonbehavioral-important.

Behavioral-Important: 4,   9, 11, 18, 20.
Behavioral-Unimportant: 2,   6, 10, 13, 17.
Nonbehavioral-Important: 1,   3, 12, 15, 16.
Nonbehavioral-Unimportant: 5,   7,   8, 14, 19.

Establishing Performance Standards

PART I.   1. S, 2. N, 3. C, 5. S, 6. N, 7. N, 8. S, 9. C, 10. N.

PART II.   11. The student will write a composition which exhibits *no spelling errors.*

12. *Ninety per cent of the students* will be able to
label *all parts of a diagram* of the human skeleton.

13. *At least 20 students* will voluntarily select poetry
books from the library.

14. *All members* of the class will participate *at least
twice* in a class discussion on foreign policy.

PART III. 15. Rewritten objective must identify level of learner
behavior desired plus proportion of class ex-
pected to master the behavior; for example, the
following would be correct: "At least 80 per cent
of the class will correctly answer 90 per cent of
the completion items on medieval England."

16. Rewritten objective must identify level of learner
behavior.desired; for example, "The student will
be able to solve at least three-fourths of the
statistics problems presented in the examination."

A Curriculum Rationale

PART I.   The following items should be checked: 1, 2, 4.

PART II. 7. D, 8. A, 9. B, 10. F, 11. C, 12. E.